J McMillen

A closer LOOK at JUNGLES

Joyce Pope

Illustrated by
Richard Orr

Hamish Hamilton · London

Jungle!

Jungle! what a world of terror the word conjures up, with wild beasts waiting to pounce lurking in every spiny thicket, poisonous snakes ready to attack, myriads of stinging and biting insects and, perhaps worst of all, spiders who may trap you in the sticky folds of their giant webs. How much truth is there in this awful vision? Like most nightmares, when looked at calmly, it turns out to be a compound of half-truths, spiced with imagination, and bears little resemblance to reality. It is true that if you go to a tropical forest, you may get the impression of a plant world waiting to engulf you with growth so vigorous that it seems malignant, but the 'green hell' of many travellers is the scene viewed from rivers or near civilisation. Close to rivers, light can filter through the trees to the ground and where man has made settlements he has felled the original forest, again letting in the light. Where these conditions of moisture, light and warmth exist, a mass of plants will struggle to survive in the space made for them. The word 'jungle' originally referred to the dense growth which occurred soon after tropical forest had been felled in India. Now it is often used to describe any sort of tropical forest in any part of the world.

What then should we call this wild luxuriance of the tropics? Unfortunately, there is no single convenient term, which is perhaps why the word 'jungle' has been so overworked. A scientist would probably say 'lowland tropical rain forest', which is a clumsy phrase but describes exactly one of the main kinds of habitat (or living place) in the world. All the words in this phrase are important: the word forest, because trees are the chief sort of plants to grow where the conditions are right for them; the word tropical, because plants of warm places are different from those in the colder parts of the world; the word lowland because on the slopes

4

and tops of mountains you would find different plants growing; and rain is important because all trees need a good deal of moisture – warm areas of low rainfall will not be covered with forest. It may rain nearly every day in some lowland tropical rain forests; in others there may be a comparatively dry season, but the forest is always a damp place, drained by great rivers, which, when they flood, leave areas of swamp behind.

In such a forest, the trees are usually very large and it is difficult to see what lives in their branches. It is only near rivers or in clearings that the forest is almost impenetrable; once through this barrier, you could walk for an hour and not see the same sort of tree twice. This is quite different from the forests of the north, where great areas may be covered with just one kind of tree. Although there are plenty of animals which make their homes in the forests, they are difficult to find, for most of them are small and solitary. At best, they live in family groups which cannot rival the huge herds of mammals of the tropical plains. Only the ants and termites seem, in some places, to live up to the travellers' tales of teeming forest life. As night falls, however, there is often a great chorus of croaks and squeaks, whistles and howls from the many animals about to begin their activities in the hours of darkness. Again, at dawn, a similar chorus heralds the emergence of the elusive creatures of the light, rarely seen by observers, so well do they match their natural background.

Inside the forest

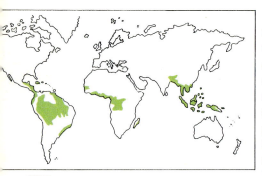

Rain forests
The great rain forests are in lowland areas of the tropics, in South America, West and Central Africa and south east Asia.

Once the wall of growth which fringes the banks of tropical rivers or surrounds any clearing has been breached, the true forest turns out to be a very different place from what you might have expected. Walking here is not difficult, for the trees are well spaced out and there is little growth on the ground – unless you come to a place where a giant tree has fallen, and here you will find the same jungle vegetation as at the forest's edge. There is no wind at ground level, and the stillness makes the forest seem an eerie place. Shielded by the mat of high growth – for the branches may not spring from the trunks until more than 30 metres above your head – your main danger will be in losing your way, for the sun will be totally hidden by the spreading and interlacing branches above you.

The forest seems to make its own climate. Even in areas away from the Equator, where the effects of seasons are beginning to be generally felt, the inside of the forest will remain warm and humid throughout the year. There is no time when the trees are bare of leaves, for there is no winter resting period as in other climates. Trees may shed their leaves at any time and having done so, grow new ones immediately. As all the plants seem to live to their own timetable, there is no moment at which all are leafless at once. As a result, you feel yourself, in the forest, to be walking in a cathedral, dimly lit, with the great buttressed tree trunks stretching up like pillars towards the distant green roof. Scrambling over the trees and hanging from their branches are the rope-like stems of climbing plants or lianas, and the aerial roots of plants growing on the trees themselves but trying to reach the ground for more sustenance. Underfoot is a carpet of dead leaves, adding to the forest's sombre appearance, which is broken only occasionally by vividly coloured ground fungi.

Green world
The tropical forest is a green world (far right). The only flashes of colour occur near rivers or in clearings where small flowering trees or shrubs may bloom, like Strelizia (right). Occasionally a brilliantly coloured butterfly like the Helicon (above) may dart down to the lower layers from the sunlit canopy.

Anatomy of a rain forest

A bird flying over a tropical rain forest would see below it an unbroken sea of green. Like the real oceans, this sea would not be still, for the canopy of the forest is in constant, slight movement from the wind. In some places it would seem as though this had thrown up great 'waves', but these would be the very tallest trees, or 'emergents', which in the forests of south east Asia may reach a height of 70 metres. In other areas the tallest trees are somewhat smaller than this, but they are always huge by temperate forest standards. Below the level of the emergents is the continuous cover of the forest canopy. This is usually at a height of over 30 metres above the ground. It would be invisible from the air because of the denseness of its leafy topping.

A human walking on the ground could not even see the underside of the canopy completely for an understory of smaller plants. Some of these are saplings of the forest giants; a few are small trees. All carry a load of woody climbers or lianas on their trunks and branches as well as smaller herbaceous plants, all competing in their upward struggle towards the light. Between them, these layers of vegetation blot out the light from the forest floor so that, apart from a few fungi and mosses, hardly anything grows there.

Indistinct boundaries

Botanists name layers of tropical rain forest but it is difficult to distinguish these in practice. In the cross-section below, however, the tallest emergent tree can be seen poking through the canopy layer of next tallest trees. Like most canopy trees, the emergent has buttressed roots; a tree on the right has long stilt roots. These devices support the tall trunks with their top-heavy crowns in the shallow soil. There may be no clear division between the canopy and middle layer trees, like the palms here, and all are linked by the lianas which wind from layer to layer. On the far left, a giant tree has fallen, allowing lower level plants to flourish in the sunlight. Tall tree saplings will shoot up to fill this gap.

Canopy layer

Tall canopy trees adopt special strategies to distribute their seeds. Some, like the kapok (right), have light, fluffy seeds which can float for long distances. Others like the Cannonball tree of South America have huge, heavy seeds able to crash to the ground through the thick foliage.

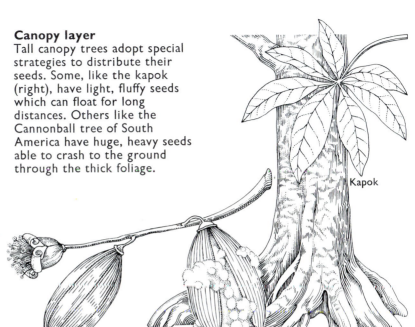

Kapok

Middle and herb layers

The oil palm, right, is a middle layer tree. Its long trunk shoots straight up and breaks out into spreading leaves designed to catch any available light. The arrowroot is a plant of the lower, herb layer which can only flourish in a clearing or near a river where there is light.

Arrowroot

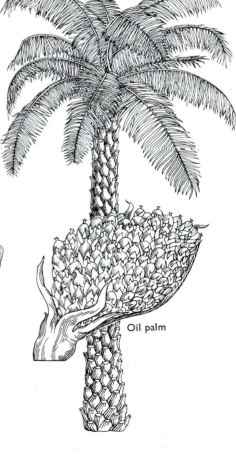

Oil palm

9

Aroid (arum)

Fern
Drynaria

Bromeliad

Bromeliad

Elkhorn fern
Platycerium

Lichen

10   Lichen

Plants on trees

The forest floor is too gloomy for there ever to be a covering of flowers such as you find in temperate woodlands in springtime. The only flowering plants are saprophytes, which are pale, leafless things, getting their nourishment from dead wood in the soil. But many plants exist and survive by using the trunks and branches of the giant forest trees to support themselves up to the light. The seedlings of such plants may look feeble, but many of them grow very fast, in some cases twining round the trunk of a big tree, in others fastening themselves to the bark with gripping rootlets. Many put down long aerial roots towards the soil, from which food and moisture may be passed up to the scrambler. Climbers such as these are unwelcome guests to the trees, which in their young stages deter the usurpers with a dense growth of spines on their main stems. For the climbers may, when they have finally reached the upper layers, smother and kill their hosts.

Other less harmful plants also grow on trees. In the dense shade, near the ground these may be small filmy ferns and mosses which need little light. Higher up a host of bigger plants thrive. They rarely do any harm for most of them are epiphytes – plants which live on other plants merely for support, not nourishment. They establish themselves on the branches either by growing from very tiny seeds or spores wafted by air currents, or from seeds deposited by birds cleaning their beaks after eating sticky fruits. Many kinds of orchids, usually ground plants, and mistletoe, grow in this way. Some of them are known as air plants, for they seem to need so little to survive, but lack of water is one of their most serious problems. Many form cup-like rosettes of leaves which act as reservoirs in the dry season. To defend themselves against damage by plant-eating insects such as cockroaches, some epiphytes offer a home to ants, which eat or drive off any creature attacking the plants.

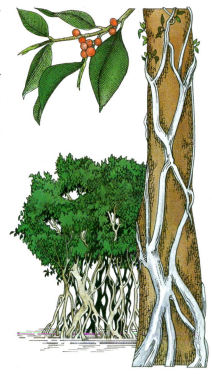

Strangler figs
These grow from seeds deposited by birds or the wind on tree branches. They send down aerial roots which enclose the host tree, gradually killing it. The fig survives, standing on its pillar of lacy roots.

Pink orchid
Cattleya

Purple orchid
Zygopetalum

Orange orchid
Maxilleria

Moss

Great black cockatoo

African grey parrot

Violet sabre-wing hummingbird

Gold and blue macaw

Ruby-throated hummingbird

Sword-billed hummingbird

Fruit- and nectar-feeders
Parrots have strong beaks to crack nuts and seeds and tear fruit. Hummingbirds (right) have long bills and tongues for sipping nectar.

Flying mammals of the forest
Bats have adopted flight as the best way to move through the trees. Below is a fruit bat and right a long-tongued bat (1) (a nectar-feeder), a fishing bat (2) and vampire bats (3).

A three-dimensional world

Toucan
New World

All of the great tropical forests are found in areas where the climate has changed little over millions of years. Many kinds of plants and animals have developed in this time to fit their environment very completely. Although they may be difficult to see from the ground, the forest is the home of more kinds of plants and animals per square kilometre than any other of the world's living places. The reason for this is that it is a three-dimensional world and few of the animals are bound to remain at any one level for any length of time. Earth-bound creatures such as horses or kangaroos must stay on the ground – a monkey, living among the trees, may move through 50 metres in its daily search for food or sleeping places, or even more if it is attempting to escape from enemies, and this will represent only a fraction of the forest's living space. The canopy and the middle layers are the richest parts of the environment, but there is no space which is completely unused. Even the insides of the tree trunks and their bark are homes to many sorts of grub.

One reason for the large number of different species is that animals have become completely specialised to particular parts of the forest. Among mosquitoes for example, different species are to be found on the ground from those inhabiting the middle and upper layers of the trees. Each group keeps to its own habitat, the tree-living ones laying their eggs in water which has collected at the base of the leaves of certain plants, or in rot holes in the branches or trunks. Each species flies, feeds and mates at a particular time of day or night, so that competition for food and living space is reduced to a minimum. For larger animals, food and shelter are always available and as there is no need to travel far to find a tree in fruit or flower, there are none of the spectacular migrations which are found among animals of cooler climates.

Hornbill
Old World

Convergent evolution
This occurs when animals from different continents, like those above, grow to look alike because they lead such similar lives.

Moving through the trees

Moving through the trees is not difficult for animals which can fly. Apart from insects, birds and bats, all of which have true flapping flight, many other jungle animals have evolved the ability to travel through the air, mostly by gliding. Best at this are animals with a gliding membrane or *patagium*, which is a flap of skin stretched between the fore and hind feet and, in some cases, further extended from the neck to the wrists and from the hind feet to the end of the tail. The most effective gliders of this kind can travel over 75 metres through the trees. They leap from a trunk or branch, spreading their limbs so that the flying membrane is stretched out like a paper dart. As they glide, they lose a little height but they recover this when they swoop upwards to land.

Other four-legged animals have developed the ability to climb and many of the forest creatures, even those which normally live on the ground, can if need be scramble out of danger. Some of the climbers are very agile and acrobatic especially those, like the monkeys, the kinkajou and the tree-climbing pangolins, with prehensile tails which they can use as extra hands to hang on with – some New World monkeys can support themselves entirely in this way. Many of these fast-moving climbers have eyes which point

Sharp claws for climbing
Tree-living South American iguanas live in the canopy where they are camouflaged perfectly, feeding on flowers and foliage.

Acrobats of the forest
In the forests of the islands off south east Asia, the orang utan (1) moves slowly and carefully in the lower branches. Gibbons (2) brachiate (swing rapidly from arm to arm) through the tree tops – where their cousins, macaques (3) and silvered langurs (4) also leap about with agility. The spectral tarsiers (5) are specialised leapers with friction pads on their toes. Another primate, the slow loris (6) moves slowly from handhold to handhold. The palm squirrel (7) and jungle cat (8) use their claws for climbing. On the ground, the little chevrotain (9) freezes when danger threatens, while the jungle fowl (10) flies up into the branches.

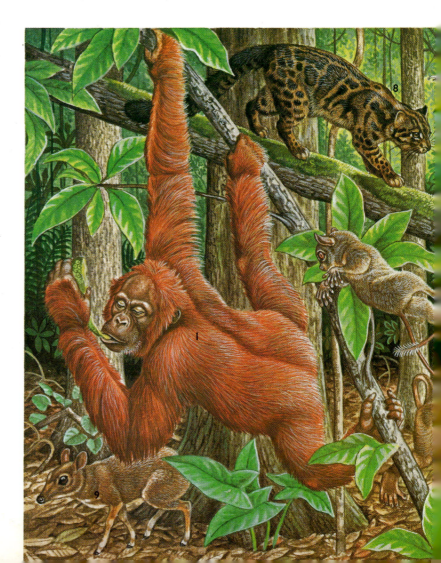

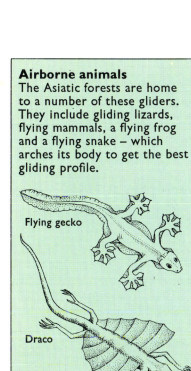
forwards so that they can judge distances well. Even so, the best of forest acrobats may fall – a survey of gibbons has shown that many of them suffer broken limbs at some time, presumably because they have missed a hand or foothold. Other animals such as squirrels and lizards have sharp toe-nails which they use as climbing irons to dig into the bark of trees. These creatures can scamper quite quickly along branches and up and down tree trunks, but they rarely attempt to jump far or onto a slender hold, for their claws might slip. Some frogs and lizards have sucker-like feet, which enable them to move over smooth foliage like that of palm trees without slipping. Yet other animals have taken a quite different line and become very inactive. They include the lorises and pottos, which grasp the branches very deliberately and do not release their hold until the next foot is securely anchored. Best known of the slow-coaches of the forests are the sloths, which hang motionless by their great hooked toe-nails from the branches of canopy trees, rarely moving from one tree for years. Although they may seem vulnerable to predators in this situation, in fact they are camouflaged by green algae growing on their coats which blend in with the surrounding vegetation.

3

7

4

6

10

Living in the canopy

Although the boundaries of the forest levels are indistinct, most kinds of animals tend to remain in a fairly narrow height range. The upper canopy and the tops of the emergent trees are the home for many strange creatures. They are mostly small, lightweight and active, for slow, heavy animals would be at a disadvantage trying to balance on the topmost twigs. Leaves, flowers and fruits here provide an ample diet for many kinds of insect. These, in turn, are food for bats, small mammals like the agile little mouse opossum, many birds and some monkeys. In the canopy, as elsewhere in the jungle, you can see how the lives of the forest dwellers are linked together: some birds – hummingbirds in the Americas and sunbirds in the Old World – feed on nectar and act as pollinators of plants at the same time; many other birds feed on fruit but often leave much of the soft pulp uneaten so that it is available for less powerful fruit eaters, including smaller birds and insects. Monkeys may feed on fruit, insects or birds' eggs but they themselves are preyed on by birds, for the biggest predators of the tree tops of both Old and New World tropical forests are large carnivorous birds like the monkey-eating eagle of South America, which is quick to seize any unwary small mammal or reptile.

A South American canopy
There are many species in the jungle but only a few representatives of each, and this is true of the canopy as well. The branches here cannot support heavy animals; the largest predator, a monkey-eating eagle swoops on a band of squirrel monkeys while howlers look on from above. A slow-moving sloth feeds on leaves. A prehensile-tailed opossum and a tree snake hunt for small prey. Gaudy macaws and a brilliant morpho butterfly flit through the canopy. A giant mantis waits patiently for an unwary insect to approach. The spectacular caterpillar will deter predators with its display of spines while the thorn shield bug may escape attack by its bizarre disguise.

The lower canopy

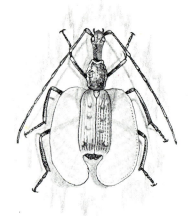

Ghostly ground beetle
Ground beetles are voracious hunters of other insects. Camouflaged against a tree trunk, this beetle can surprise its prey and avoid being eaten itself.

Creatures of the understory
The world under the canopy is a busy one. The understory provides a travelling way for many animals. Monkeys, birds, bats and winged insects move up and down through its branches in a constant two-way traffic in search of food. Leaves, bark and branches provide food and homes for many insects – grubs, wasps, bees, leaf crickets, ants and termites. In turn, the rich variety of insect life means plenty to eat for insectivores like birds and bats and specialised feeders like the smaller anteaters, which clamber among the branches, searching out the nests of tree ants and termites.

1. Wrinkle-faced bats
2. Red-beaked wasp
3. Brown leaf long-horned grasshopper
4. Huge brown stick insect
5. Tamandua (anteater)
6. Triangular-winged disruptive noctuid moth
7. Green and white patterned noctuid moth
8. Grape shoemaker butterfly
9. Notodontid moth
10. Leaf long-horned grasshopper
11. Chestnut woodpecker

The lower canopy and the understory layers of the forest are perhaps the richest of all in life. Here the dense tangle of branches takes the last remnant of light from above, but gives more food and shelter to a wide range of animals: most of the monkeys and sloths live here, for example. Some of the trees are in decay and their hollow trunks and rotting branches are home to myriads of animals. Many of the forest birds nest in the safety of such places, where they may be able to hide from the attacks of tree snakes and other predators. Some, like the African hornbills, may take natural hollows in trees for their nests. In other species, the female bird is literally walled up with the eggs and nestlings until they are ready to fly. The male has the sole duty of feeding his wife and nestlings. Other kinds of birds, such as woodpeckers, prefer to take a branch weakened by decay and excavate a custom-built hole in it for their nursery. These holes may be used later by other birds, like parrots, or other small animals for resting places. Rotting wood provides food for insects particularly beetle grubs. One of the most spectacular of all forest insects, the harlequin beetle, spends the early years of its life breaking down decaying trees.

Brilliantly-coloured butterflies flap lazily about the lower layers

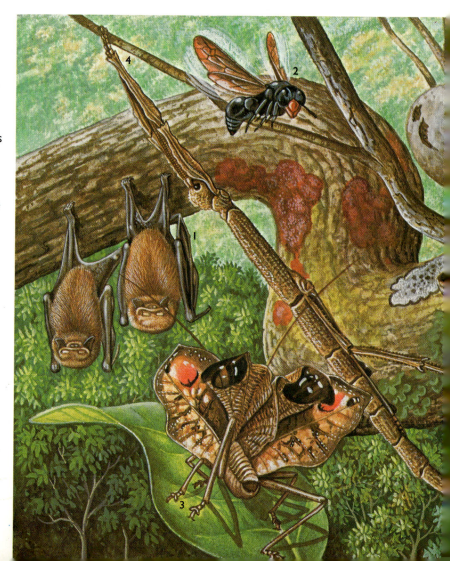

of the forest. At first they may seem to be of few kinds but, as so often in this complex world, things are not what they seem. Frequently, several species look so much alike that they could well be mistaken for each other. This form of mimicry has a practical purpose for some of the butterflies will taste nasty and a bird or a lizard which has experienced the foul flavour of one will avoid the others.

While some ants and termites live and nest in the trees, others, such as the fungus garden ants, only climb the twigs to cut pieces of leaf which they carry back to their nest on the ground. Here the leaf fragments are used to make a compost heap on which the ants grow the special fungi which are their food.

Many other insects are perfectly camouflaged to match the background on which they sit. Some are shaped like twigs, leaves or thorns; others match the bark or the lichens which grow on the tree trunks in colour and texture. These creatures are active at night, when a different group of animals takes over in the forest. This day and night shift system, owls replacing hawks, bats flying instead of birds, and moths in place of butterflies, ensures that all the resources of the environment are used as fully as possible.

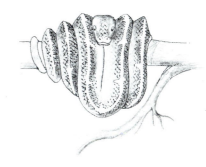

Emerald boa
Many snakes are adapted to life in the trees. This beautiful boa waits motionless for an unwary animal to come within its range. The emerald boa is a constrictor and is not poisonous although other tree snakes, like African mambas, are.

19

The forest litter

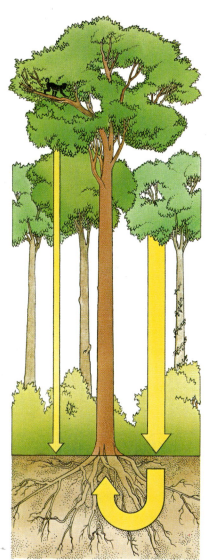

Although the forest floor looks sombre and dull compared to the colour and activity of the branches above, it is on this part of the habitat that the life of the whole area depends, for here we find the recycling system of the forest. The trees drop their leaves to the ground in a steady shower throughout the year. Once they are on the ground, they are attacked by a multitude of organisms, all of which tend to break them down to their constituent minerals, so that the soil is enriched and the trees and other big plants can continue to get nourishment from it. The most obvious of these scavenging organisms are the fungi. The fruiting bodies of the toadstools are often short-lived, but their thread-like mycelial strands are busy under the leaf litter doing their job of breaking down the organic substances they need for food. Also invisible, because of their small size, bacteria and protozoa help to digest the tough leaves, aided by worms, mites, millipedes and springtails.

Fallen logs, the last remnants of the kings of the forest, are home, as they decompose, for a series of grubs, woodlice, snails and slugs. In its last stages of decay a log may provide food for the larvae of the giant hercules beetle. Tree ants and termites live in small groups but most of those found in the leaf litter form vast colonies.

Two of the strangest creatures found in tropical forest soils are the velvet worm, a kind of living fossil showing us an ancient link between the worms and the insects, and giant flatworms. These small creatures normally live in water but in the moist forest soils some of them grow to a gigantic size of over 10 centimetres.

The turnover of energy in the soil is not a direct one, but has stages in which hunters feed on scavengers. Carnivorous beetles and bugs feed on smaller grubs and are themselves food for frogs, birds, shrews or other small mammals.

Decomposition (above)
In the moist, warm tropical forests, dead animal and vegetable matter which falls to the forest floor is rapidly broken down and washed into the soil. Here the minerals it contains are reabsorbed through the roots of the trees and help new growth which, in turn, falls and decays, continuing the cycle.

Creatures of the forest floor
1. Millipede
2. Planiarium
3. Centipede
4. Lantern fly
5. Peripetatus
6. Leech
7. Giant hercules beetle
8. Phoebus butterflies
9. Horned frog

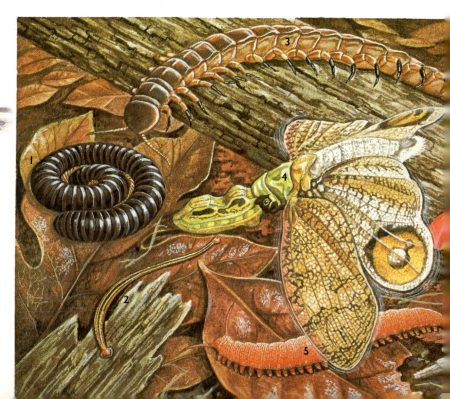

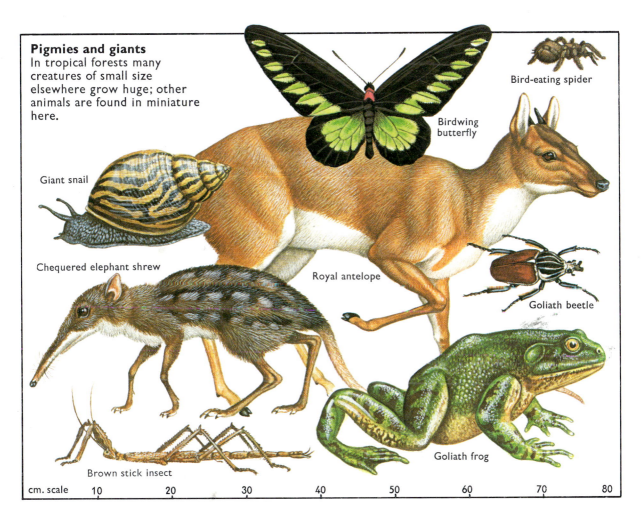

Pigmies and giants
In tropical forests many creatures of small size elsewhere grow huge; other animals are found in miniature here.

Birdwing butterfly

Bird-eating spider

Giant snail

Chequered elephant shrew

Royal antelope

Goliath beetle

Goliath frog

Brown stick insect

cm. scale 10   20   30   40   50   60   70   80

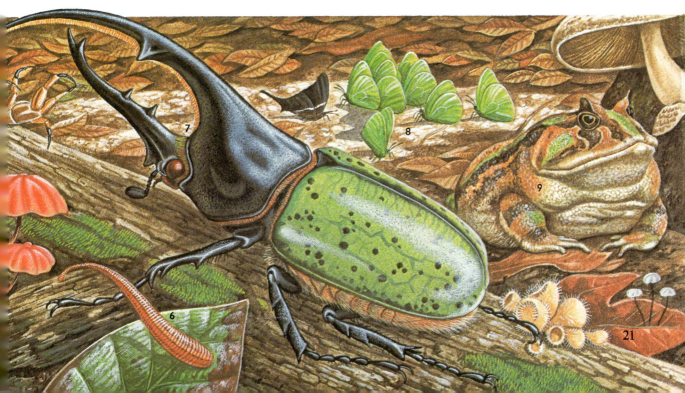

7

8

9

6

Ground dwellers

Leopard

Jaguar

Tiger

Great predators
In the Asiatic forests, tigers hunt on the ground and leopards in the trees. The New World jaguar hunts in both places and looks like a rather clumsily built leopard.

The main riches of the forest are to be found high above the ground but there is little here in the way of food for big animals. As might be expected few of them live in the deep forest for it is only in clearings and near to rivers that there is enough for them to eat. Since these areas are likely to be flooded for part of each year, this restricts the living space still further.

In Africa, the forest elephant, a subspecies of the common African form, lives under the cover of the trees. Chimpanzees and gorillas, although well able to climb, especially when young, spend much of their time on the ground, except when in danger or looking for a place to sleep. The shy okapi is an inhabitant of the thick forest. The bongo, a large antelope, is found in the same habitat along with various small hoofed animals, including chevrotains and duikers. These animals are all solitary, or at best live in pairs, and browse on the leaves of shrubs, on fungi and on fallen fruits.

In the forests of South America, nuts and seeds form almost the whole diet of the tapir and the roaming herds of pig-like peccaries. Among the smaller mammals of this area are guinea pigs, which hide in hollow logs during the daytime and emerge at night to enjoy the fruit and nuts which have fallen from the tall trees.

The strangest animals of the forest floor are those which feed on ants and termites. Pangolins in the Old World and anteaters in the New, harvest the teeming populations of these insects, using their great claws to tear open the nests and long, sticky tongues to lap up the hoards which run madly round to protect their citadel.

Besides the mammals, many birds scratch and hunt for plant or insect food beneath the trees. But all may fall prey to flesh-eating mammals, mainly members of the cat family – jaguars in America and leopards in the Old World, as well as numerous smaller hunting cats like ocelots or servals.

An 'outsize guinea pig'
The shy, water-loving capybara is the world's largest rodent. Living by forest streams and swamps, it rushes into the water if attacked by men or jaguars.

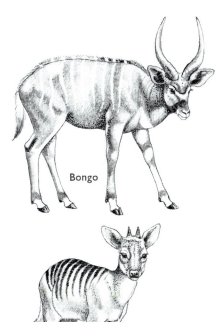

Bongo

Banded duiker

Camouflage
The shy, well-camouflaged okapi (right) was the last large African animal to be discovered. Also well hidden in dappled foliage are the two African antelopes above.

Rare mammal
All the Asiatic rhinoceroses are threatened with extinction, particularly the Javan and Sumatran species, now the rarest large land animals in the world.

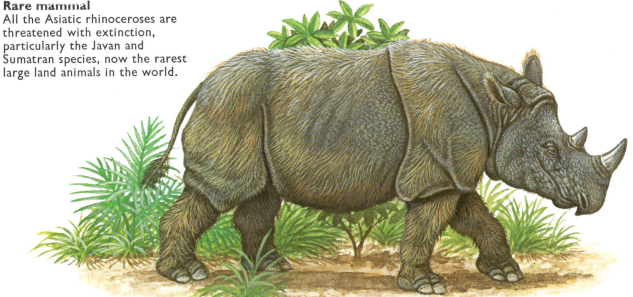

River life

All lowland tropical forests are carved through by huge rivers, their size almost unbelievable in terms of temperate landscapes. For most of its length the River Amazon is over 8 kilometres wide; as it nears the sea, its width increases to more than 300 kilometres. In those parts where there is a definite rainy season, great areas of forest may be flooded each year. Most of the forest animals can climb out of the way of the encroaching waters, or else they are good swimmers. When the waters retreat, the rivers often change course, leaving behind ox-bow lakes and swamps, which are the homes of frogs and salamanders, reptiles and birds, as well as many insects which begin their lives in the water.

All the time, the rivers are gradually undermining their banks and they carry off trees and creepers and waterside grasses in great tangled mats. Sometimes these form the bases for islands.

From the river, the land seems impenetrable. In many places, tall grasses stand in the water, backed by pallisades of arums, and behind these there is the scrambling, spiny growth of many plants competing for the light. Here one of the Amazon's strangest birds is found, the hoatzin. Nesting close to the water, the chicks are at risk if they fall, but they are saved by the long fingers on their unfeathered wings which enable them to grasp the vegetation and scramble back home.

A vast array of fishes lives in the waters. There is even an Amazon fish which feeds on fruits which have fallen into the river. Others feed on water plants while others again are hunters. Some, like the leaf fish, rely on stealth. It floats downstream, looking like a dead leaf in the water until it is near enough to its prey to engulf it. The hunters include the fierce piranha.

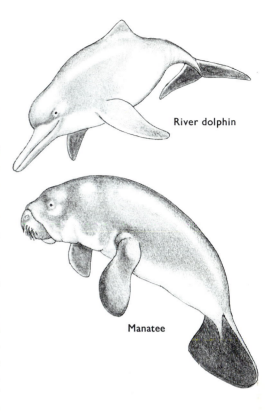

River dolphin

Manatee

Water mammals
The major river systems of tropical forests contain large, water-living mammals like river dolphins and the sluggish manatees (sea cows) of the Amazon.

The hunter hunted
An Amazon caiman struggles in the coils of an anaconda. Spoonbills and a river turtle watch from the bank. The fish, from left to right, are tetras, *Leporhinus*, piranha and arawana.

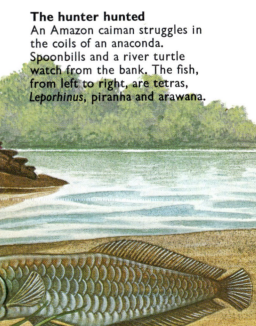

25

Forest people

Man, the cleverest and most adaptable of all animals, has made his home in the tropical rain forests. There are still native peoples in the great rain forests, but the life described here is restricted increasingly to a dwindling number of groups and tribes. Forest indians have usually lived in fairly small settlements, near to a river which could be used for transport – they were often expert at making and using canoes. They could also fish in the river if necessary or they could go into the forest to hunt or collect fruit. Human populations usually remained small and were mostly organised on a tribal basis. In Asia and Africa, the people of tropical forest areas are of very small build and the pigmies of Malaysia and the Congo are the smallest of all human races. In South America, the forest people are compactly built but are not pigmies.

The hunting techniques of the forest peoples always involved stealth and they moved quietly up to their prey and shot it with small bows and arrows or, in some areas, a dart projected from a blow pipe. By this almost silent method of hunting, several animals could be killed where the use of guns would almost certainly have meant that less food would be caught. Fish usually formed

Hunting for food
To make sure of killing his prey, an Amazon indian dipped his arrow head in poison (if the prey ran off, only wounded, it might never be found in the jungle). The poison used was the skin secretion of small frogs. Other poisons with antidotes were also used to capture not kill animals.

Food plants

Forest plants fruit all the year round so food from them was not hard to find. Roots like yams and cassava could be pounded into 'flour'. Lack of salt was partly made up for by adding a variety of wild spices and herbs to tropical food.

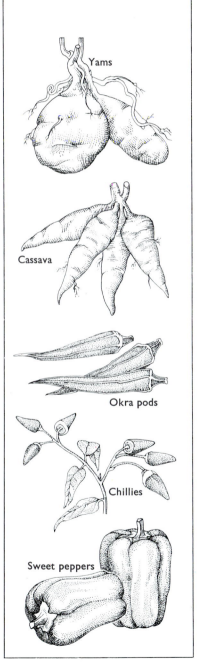

Yams

Cassava

Okra pods

Chillies

Sweet peppers

an important part of the diet and were speared or shot, netted or trapped according to the custom of the tribe.

All of the indians' needs had to be supplied from the forest: food and drink, plants for medicinal use and dyes, fibres for ropes and wood for canoes. Even insects and their grubs formed an important part of the food of some people. Some tribes cultivated small patches of ground. In South America, cassava was a favourite crop, for not only did the pith of this small tree produce wholesome food, but the crop grew easily with very little attention required and could be left in the ground for up to two years without harm. Fruit from some of the big forest trees was eaten but smaller plants, more accessible for harvesting, were generally more useful – although the guava, mango and palm trees were valuable food sources. Perhaps the avocado pear, which has a high protein and fat content was the most valuable but the fruit of another small tree, the pawpaw, was said to have medicinal properties and coca beans were chewed as a stimulant. Some of the waterside scrambling plants, such as melons and gourds, were harvested and so was the yam – a root-like tuber. By our standards, the forest was a hard world; it was a place where man, if he was to survive, had to merge totally and become part of the pattern of nature.

Shifting cultivation

Forest people practised a method of agriculture which involved cutting down trees over a small area, letting them dry and then burning them. For a few seasons crops could be grown in the ash-enriched soil then the farmers would move on to another part of the forest to repeat the process. Right, are indians harvesting sweet potatoes.

Man the exploiter

The coming of white men with modern technology to the great forests of the world has spelt disaster to what must, at first, have seemed like a limitless, stable environment. To begin with, the inroads were small and confined to taking timber from accessible places. Later, large areas were felled and often whole forests were destroyed. In small areas, such as on some islands, destruction was horrifyingly rapid. It is said that after the island of Barbados was discovered, all of its native forests were totally destroyed within forty years. The island is now far from treeless but such species as grow there have all been introduced. Many valuable species have become extinct through over-exploitation, like the fine Spanish mahogany, totally logged out of the forests of the West Indies.

But the story has not been entirely one of removal. Where crops have seemed useful, forest plants have been taken from one area to another, to form plantations and crop plants. Bananas were carried from the East Indies to Africa and the West Indies; rubber trees made the journey from South America to the Far East; Captain Bligh was carrying a cargo of breadfruit plants from Tahiti to the West Indies when the crew of his ship the *Bounty* mutinied and cast him adrift. A list of all the plant movements of the last 200 years would be immense. As a result of them, we now find forest plants grown as crops – often in areas long since cleared of their own forest – and many tropical plants scattered throughout the warmer parts of the globe. There is no doubt that many people have benefited from this. The losers have been the original inhabitants of the forests, both man and animal, which have disappeared before the tide of civilisation and, once gone, cannot be recalled.

Forestry
Nowadays tropical timber is felled selectively, so that there is a chance for young trees to grow and old ones to regenerate within the forest framework.

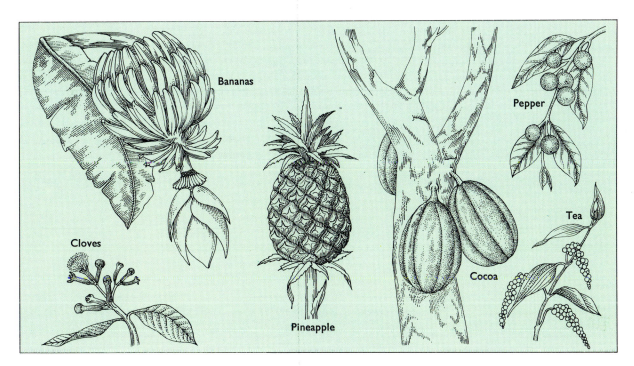

Bananas

Pepper

Cloves

Tea

Pineapple

Cocoa

Cash crops

The cash crops grown on the site of old forests include many plants which are of forest origin. Palms for coconuts and oil, cocoa and bananas are all examples. In general, they are grown as monoculture crops, so that the unrivalled diversity once found in the forest has vanished. It is possible that, with better storage and transport, more tropical fruits will find their way into the great urban markets of the world. The market for all of the crops illustrated here could be enlarged, bringing further prosperity to parts of the tropics.

A bleak tomorrow

The future of the great forests of the world looks bleak at the moment. The coming of man with high technology to areas which had previously known only small populations of people with primitive cultures, has meant that both the forests and their inhabitants have fallen back before the onslaught. This takes several forms. First is the direct one: the felling of the original forest and its replacement with some sort of agriculture. This is almost always accompanied by reprisals against the people of the forest, who resent the taking of what they see as their lands by strangers, and who try to resist the change. Nowhere has this been more savagely accomplished than in South America, where the indians have been destroyed in a variety of ways, resulting in the extinction of many tribes which only a century ago seemed to be flourishing. The animals of the forest have fared no better. Many creatures have been brought to the verge of extinction by the demands of the pet or the fur trade. Although both of these are now somewhat curtailed, in some cases at least it may be that the damage is irreparable. Certainly a large number of forest animals, plentiful until recently, now appear in the Red Data Book of threatened species.

Whether this destruction can be halted is doubtful. The call for more food for more humans is a powerful one, although we now know something of the part played in climatic control by the great forests which should make us pause and think what we are doing in destroying them. In most forest areas, there are already parts set aside as national parks or reserves. Although these are tiny compared to the original forests, they may form a nucleus from which reafforestation some day may take place. So there is hope that, while the forests may be altered, they will not disappear altogether for many years to come.

Return to forest

Not everywhere cleared by man is suitable for crops or replanting so in some areas of what was once tropical rain forest, waste land is returning to the wild. The riot of secondary plant growth which springs up here is the kind which once characterised forest clearings. This 'jungle' is not true forest and the animals of the area have gone for ever but, given enough time, it will eventually be overtopped by the great trees of tropical rain forest.

31

Index